D1558284

Your Florida Guide to Butterfly Gardening

Also in this series
Your Florida Guide to Bedding Plants
Your Florida Guide to Shrubs

Companion Video
Butterfly Gardening in Florida
(available from IFAS Publications)

YOUR FLORIDA GUIDE TO BUTTERFLY GARDENING

A Guide for the Deep South

Jaret C. Daniels

Institute of Food and Agricultural Sciences (IFAS)
University of Florida

University Press of Florida
Gainesville · Tallahassee · Tampa · Boca Raton
Pensacola · Orlando · Miami · Jacksonville

The companion video to this book is available from:
   IFAS Publications Distribution Center
   P.O. Box 110011
   Gainesville, Florida 32611–0011
   1–800–226–1764 (Orders only please; MasterCard and Visa accepted.)

Library of Congress Cataloging-in-Publication Data

Designer: Larry Leshan
Illustrations: Jane Medley
Photography: Jaret C. Daniels
Editor: Charles Brown

The University of Florida's Institute of Food and Agricultural Sciences (IFAS) brings
together the forces of the College of Agriculture, the Florida Cooperative Extension
Service, the Agriculture Experiment Station at the University of Florida, and the
statewide network of Research and Education Centers. The research, education, and
extension efforts of IFAS improve the lives of almost everyone in the state from the
homeowner to huge agribusiness operations in such areas as food safety, gardening,
child and family development, consumer credit counseling, youth development, energy
conservation, sustainable agriculture, competitiveness in world markets, and natural
resource conservation. Look into IFAS—visit our Web site at: http://ifas.ufl.edu

The University Press of Florida is the scholarly publishing agency for the State University
System of Florida, comprising Florida A&M University, Florida Atlantic University,
Florida International University, Florida State University, University of Central Florida,
University of Florida, University of North Florida, University of South Florida, and
University of West Florida.

University Press of Florida
15 NW 15th Street
Gainesville, Florida 32611–2079
http://www.upf.com

CONTENTS

INTRODUCTION

Planting a butterfly garden is a simple and rewarding way to experience a bit of wild Florida. Unlike most wildlife, butterflies are not confined to remote, natural areas. They are a common sight in both country and city and can easily be attracted with a little know-how and the proper planning.

Whether it fits in a container on the patio or stretches over several acres, a well-planned butterfly garden can be as simple or as complicated as you want to make it. The same basic concepts and guidelines apply whatever the size. The most important thing to understand before you begin is that butterflies have many different behaviors, affinities, and needs; however, these requirements often change dramatically throughout their life cycle. A well-planned butterfly garden should provide variety to attract different kinds of butterflies and cater to both adult butterflies and their larvae. Proper choice of plants and landscape design is essential. Such decisions will help determine which butterfly species will be attracted, remain in the area, and ultimately reproduce.

Planting a butterfly garden does not mean sacrificing your landscape style or individual preferences to the needs of butterflies. Nor does it mean turning your yard into a glorified weed patch. A well-designed butterfly garden can be very formal, wildly naturalistic, or any point in between. It can take the form of a new garden or a simple modification of an existing landscape. The choice is yours.

A Note about Scientific Names

Throughout this book, you will see the common names of butterflies and plants followed by their scientific names, such as: Spicebush Swallowtail *(Papilio troilus)*. A scientific name identifies a particular species of plant or animal. Although most people become familiar with names like Monarch butterfly and Pawpaw shrub, these common names vary from place to place and certainly from country to country. Scientists and other professionals, such as nursery owners, use scientific names for plants and animals because the scientific name is agreed upon throughout the world. Maybe it seems complicated, but it allows people to talk about plants and animals without confusion.

This system of naming is called "binomial nomenclature," meaning that every organism has two names. The first part of the name refers to the genus, and like a person's last name, shows what organisms are most closely related. Organisms with the same genus are very closely related. The second part of the name, called the "specific epithet," is like a person's first name; it refers to a particular member of the genus. For example, from their common names, you would not know that Virginia Snakeroot and Dutchman's Pipe are related, but when you see their scientific names, *Aristolochia serpentaria* and *Aristolochia macrophylla*, you know immediately that these plants are members of the same genus.

Genera (the plural of genus) can be grouped together into families. Take a look at the section "Guide to Common Florida Butterflies" and you'll see how various butterfly species are grouped into families.

WHY BUTTERFLIES ARE IMPORTANT

Butterflies are by far the most popular of all insects worldwide. Besides being attractive and providing us with a great deal of enjoyment, they play a number of important roles in the environment.

1. Butterflies help pollinate a wide range of native and cultivated flowering plants.

2. Butterflies provide food for many other organisms. A variety of small mammals, nesting birds, lizards, spiders, and other insects all feed on adult butterflies or their larvae.

An Orange Sulphur (*Colias eurytheme*) sips nectar from a Purple Coneflower blossom.

Spiders are common garden predators. While they do occasionally capture and eat butterflies, they are highly beneficial organisms and will not adversely affect the butterfly numbers in your garden.

Bartram's Hairstreak (*Strymon acis bartrami*), left, and the Florida Leafwing Butterfly (*Anaea floridalis*), above, are rare residents of south Florida's pine rockland habitat.

The tiny Swedner's Hairstreak (*Mitoura gryneus swedneri*) is an infrequent sight throughout north-central regions of the state. The butterfly is completely dependent upon Southern Red Cedar, its sole larval host plant.

3. Due to their tremendous appeal and popularity, butterflies often serve as "umbrella" species. When butterflies are protected, their habitats and the other creatures that live there are also protected. The endangered Schaus Swallowtail in south Florida is a good example. Efforts to save this spectacular butterfly have received a great deal of public support and attention. As a result, the globally endangered tropical hardwood hammock habitat the Schaus Swallowtail calls home and the other organisms that live there have benefited from the conservation efforts and increased visibility.

4. Butterflies are indicator species. That means they are among the first organisms to show a negative reaction to environmental changes and pollutants. Just like a canary in a coal mine, butterflies can help alert us to problems in the local environment that may affect our own health and well-being.

The Schaus Swallowtail (*Papilio aristodemus ponceanus*) is Florida's only endangered butterfly. Once reduced to dangerously low numbers in the wild by mosquito control pesticides, loss of habitat, and the impact of hurricane Andrew, the Schaus Swallowtail is making a strong comeback due to the efforts of University of Florida researchers. The resulting publicity has helped raise awareness of butterfly conservation throughout the state and the rest of the nation.

BUTTERFLY GARDENING AND CONSERVATION

Butterflies and other organisms are facing an increasingly uphill battle to survive as more and more natural areas are replaced by urban development. While planting a butterfly garden will never take the place of a natural habitat, it can help you:

1. Provide many of the resources necessary to foster populations of local butterflies and other wildlife.

2. Reduce the amount of toxic chemical pesticides in the environment by employing alternative natural pest control measures.

3. Conserve water and increase local diversity by landscaping with native plants.

4. Furnish a wonderful learning environment for you and your children.

5. Become an advocate for environmental conservation.

Give butterfly gardening a try today and encourage your friends, relatives, school systems, businesses, and local municipalities to become involved. By working together we can make a difference.

THE FOUR STAGES OF
A BUTTERFLY'S LIFE

All butterflies go through a life cycle consisting of four distinct developmental stages: egg, larva, pupa, and adult. No matter what its eventual size, every butterfly begins life as a small egg. Adult females typically deposit eggs singly or in clusters on or near specific plant species. These host plants provide growing larvae with the proper nutrition they need to complete growth and development. Larval host plants may also furnish shelter, camouflage, and chemicals used for protection, courtship, and reproduction. Caterpillars (larvae) are herbivores and have very selective tastes. Each kind of butterfly larva has a favored menu of host plants. In other words, each butterfly species only feeds on specific plant species. Consequently, butterfly larvae rarely become garden pests, but that's not to say they don't have large appetites.

Butterfly larvae are highly efficient eating machines. Just like other young creatures, their job is to eat and grow. Larvae can grow at an astonishing rate, increasing in size and weight many times over before reaching maturity. To accommodate this tremendous change in proportion, each larva sheds its skin, or molts, numerous times during its life, revealing each time a new and often radically different larval skin. Once fully grown, the larva seeks a safe place to pupate. Most attach themselves to a branch, twig, or other support by spinning silk. After a short rest, the larva molts for the last time to reveal the pupa, or chrysalis. Inside, larval structures break down and reorganize to form the adult butterfly. The almost magical series of changes from egg to adult butterfly is called metamorphosis. When environmental conditions are appropriate, the pupa splits open and a brand-new adult butterfly emerges.

A female Schaus Swallowtail (*Papilio aristodemus ponceanus*) lays an egg on the new growth of a Wild Lime tree (*Zanthoxylum fagara*).

A Palamedes Swallowtail (*Papilio palamedes*) egg on Red Bay (*Persea borbonia*).

Eggs of the Georgia Satyr (*Neonympha areolatus*) on a blade of grass.

A cluster of Tawny Emperor (*Asterocampa clyton*) eggs on Sugarberry (*Celtis laevigata*).

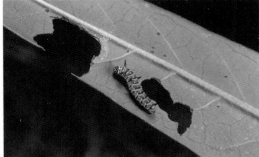

A small second instar Queen butterfly larva, now less than a 1/4 inch in length, will eventually be over 2 inches long when fully grown.

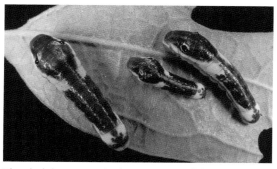

The dark brown and white pattern of these young Spicebush Swallowtail (*Papilio troilus*) larvae (left) resembles bird droppings. This drab appearance will be replaced, after molting, by the spectacular color of the fifth instar larva (right).

Suspended from a branch by silk, a mature Sleepy Orange (*Eurema nicippe*) larva will soon molt for the last time to reveal the pupa. When larvae are ready to pupate, they typically hang almost immobilized in this j-shaped posture.

Butterfly pupae come in a wide variety of shapes, sizes, and colors. Although the pupa of the Zebra Swallowtail (*Eurytides marcellus*) is brightly colored, it would be quite difficult to find among green leaves.

Above: A Tiger Swallowtail's (*Papilio glaucus*) pupa looks remarkably like a broken twig.

Right: The drab pupa of the American Painted Lady (*Vanessa virginiensis*) is wonderfully camouflaged against the silver foliage of Pearly Everlasting.

Right: A Cloudless Sulphur's (*Phoebis sennae*) pupa has a beautiful pinkish hue. The overall shape and veination of the developing butterfly's wing can be seen on the side of the pupa. When the adult is ready to emerge, both wing cases will become transparent, revealing the color of the butterfly's wings beneath.

Far right: Within an hour after emerging from its pupa, a fresh Snout Butterfly (*Libytheana bachmanii*) will be ready to take flight.

An adult butterfly's life revolves around reproduction. A male Barred Sulphur (*Eurema daira*) extends his forewing to court a resting female. He rubs specialized pheromone-producing scales on the trailing edge of his forewing against the female butterfly's antennae in an attempt to excite her and induce copulation.

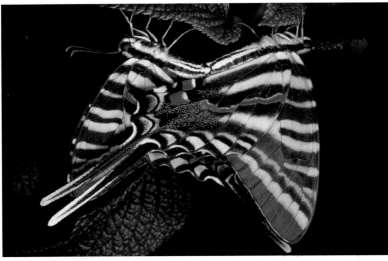

Mating butterflies are especially vulnerable to predators. Most, like this pair of Zebra Swallowtails (*Eurytides marcellus*), sit quietly on vegetation and fly only when disturbed.

BUTTERFLY GARDEN DESIGN BASICS

When the time comes to plan your butterfly garden, follow these simple and important guidelines. They will help you get the most out of your garden and attract the widest possible variety of butterfly species.

1. Provide a combination of adult nectar sources and larval host plants. Remember, a garden with both adult nectar sources and larval host plants can accommodate the entire life cycle of a butterfly. The available resources will encourage adult butterflies to remain in your yard, reproduce, and build populations year after year—not just to pass through in search of nectar.

Several Zebra Longwing (*Heliconius charitonius*) larvae feed on a passionflower vine.

A Cloudless Sulphur (*Phoebis sennae*) alights on a Mexican Sunflower.

Don't limit a butterfly garden solely to areas receiving full sun. The filtered shade of this backyard garden (above) will attract and host different butterfly species than those drawn to the blanket flowers planted in direct sunlight (right).

The placement of larval host plants can often influence how frequently they will be used by the targeted butterfly species. A Passion-vine (*Passiflora incarnata*) planted in full sun will attract many female Gulf Fritillaries (*Agraulis vanillae*). The same vine planted in a shadier area will instead be used by Zebra Longwings (*Heliconius charitionius*) and almost completely ignored by the sunny, open area–loving Gulf Fritillaries. Thus, you will need to become familiar with a butterfly's preferred habitat and plan accordingly.

2. Plant in both full sun and partial shade when available. Most butterflies and their adult nectar sources are fond of bright sunlight. However, some butterflies are at home in woodlands or along forest edges and rarely venture out into open, sunny areas. They are more often drawn to nectar sources and larval host plants located in shadier sections of the garden.

3. Aim for consistent host plant and nectar source availability throughout the growing season. Many butterflies, especially in the Deep South, are active year-round. Therefore, choose plants that bloom, grow, or perform better at different times of the year, as well as plants having one peak season. The added variety ensures that your garden will remain productive as long as possible and will provide food for butterflies during periods of low natural availability.

4. Create horizontal and vertical diversity. Choose plants that have a variety of different heights and growth habits. A diverse planting scheme adds interest and texture to the garden. It also helps to increase the number of microclimates and feeding levels available to butterflies.

5. Plant in groupings. If space allows, try to combine several plants of the same species in a large grouping. Large drifts of color and clusters of vegetation are generally more aesthetically pleasing than isolated plants. They also tend to be more apparent and attractive to adult butterflies. Groups of larval host plants provide larvae with additional resources in the event one runs out and help to mask any leaf damage or defoliation.

6. Provide a mix of flower colors, shapes, and sizes. Different butterfly species have distinct color preferences, feeding behaviors, and proboscis (tongue) lengths. Together, these factors determine which flowers a butterfly chooses or is able to visit. A wide mix of adult nectar sources provides accessible and attractive food to a greater number of butterfly species.

A large grouping of Mexican Milkweed plants (*Asclepias curassavica*) not only provides nectar for visiting adult butterflies but ample food for Monarch and Queen larvae.

Above: Many Cloudless Sulphur butterflies feed from the blooms of the Firecracker Plant (*Russelia equisetiformis*). The nectar in the downward hanging, tubular flowers is inaccessible to most other butterflies.

Top right: The butterfly garden along this driveway provides a wonderful mix of flower colors and shapes. The large drifts of individual species enhance the overall effect.

Right: Try to include as many flower colors as possible, including white.

7. Include native plants whenever possible. Unlike many culti-vated or exotic species, which perform well only under optimal conditions, native plants are well adapted to the soil type and climate of the region where they naturally occur. Consequently, once established, native plants tend to provide a more vigorous display with minimal care. They generally use less water and are not as prone to disease or pest attack. Native plants also help transform your garden into a small example of natural Florida. (Native plants are marked with an asterisk in the lists later in this book.)

8. Choose the appropriate plant for each location. Determine each plant's basic light, water, and soil requirements before planting. For example, avoid putting a sun-loving species in deep shade. A little research before you plant will ensure that your plants grow and perform to their maximum potential. When in doubt, ask about your plants at a local nursery or Extension office.

9. Look out for good weeds. Many common weeds serve as larval host plants. Carefully search each plant for larvae before you pull it out. If larvae are present, leave the plant alone until they have finished feeding. The plant can then be removed or transplanted. You may also consider leaving a small section of your garden natural.

The delicate flowers of the native Florida Azalea (*Rhododendron canescens*) are an almost irresistible spring treat for many butterflies.

10. Learn to identify the butterflies in your area. Become familiar with your local butterfly species. Try to learn which ones are common, which ones are rare, and which ones you most want to attract. Then when it is time to choose the larval host plants for your garden, gear your picks accordingly.

Many common weeds of disturbed sites are excellent butterfly plants. Sickle-pod Senna (*Cassia obtusifolia*) (left) is an important late-season larval host for the Cloudless Sulphur and the Sleepy Orange. Spanish Needles (*Bidens alba*) (below) are a superb nectar source that can easily be kept under control by pinching off the old flower heads before they go to seed.

FIVE KEYS TO A SUCCESSFUL BUTTERFLY GARDEN

Adult Nectar Sources

Adult butterflies are highly mobile and dynamic creatures. Unfortunately, most live only a few weeks. During that brief period, they must find a mate, reproduce, seek out food and shelter, and avoid being eaten—a very active schedule, to say the least. To meet these high-energy demands, most adult butterflies rely on sugar-rich nectar as fuel.

Nectar-rich, colorful flowering plants, therefore, are the backbone of any successful butterfly garden. They draw in adult butterflies from the surrounding environment like a magnet while adding beauty and interest to the landscape. They also yield almost instantaneous results. Therefore, adult nectar sources should always be the first additions to a new butterfly garden.

When selecting flower colors, aim for a variety. While reds, pinks, and purples are generally considered the most attractive adult nectar source colors, a great many butterfly species are also drawn to yellows, blues, and whites as well. As you will quickly discover, different butterfly species have distinct color preferences.

Flower shape will also influence visitation. In acquiring nectar, butterflies are limited by the length of their proboscis, or tongue. As a result, the nectar in long, tubular flowers is more accessible to butterflies possessing a longer proboscis. A butterfly's behavior while feeding affects its flower choice as well. Many large swallowtail butterflies, for example, continuously flutter their wings while nectaring. This enables them to feed much like hummingbirds, with access to flowers too delicate to land on. On the other hand, many smaller butterflies such as blues and hairstreaks prefer to feed while at rest. They are strongly attracted to large clusters of small, short-tubed flowers that form a stable platform on which to alight.

The bottom line when it comes to choosing adult nectar sources for your garden is diversity. Be creative with your selections. The greater the variety of flower colors, shapes, and sizes available, the greater variety of butterfly species will be attracted. Double and triple flowered species are the only major exception to this rule. While such flowers produce spectacular blooms, they have been bred to impress humans, not butterflies. In the process, external features have been artificially manipulated, often at the expense of nectar content or accessibility.

The bright yellow flowers of Black-eyed Susan (*Rudbecki hirta*) are wonderfully accented by the large, pink blooms of Joe-pye Weed (*Eupatorium fistulosum*) behind.

Azaleas are good spring nectar sources for a variety of sulphurs and swallowtails.

Left: A mix of flower colors and shapes is essential to attract the maximum number of butterfly species. The nectar in the long, tubular flowers of Fire Bush (*Hamelia patens*) is accessible only to butterflies with long probosces. The small, flat flower heads of *Eupatorium* "chocolate," though, provide a bounty of available food for short-tongued butterfly species.

Below: Some butterflies, like this Tiger Swallowtail (*Papilio glaucus*), flutter while they feed. As a result, they can gain access to the nectar in a wider variety of flowers.

Numerous butterflies need to rest on flowers while feeding. The many small blooms of White Swamp Milkweed (*Asclepias perennis*) make a perfect platform for this tiny Ceraunus Blue (*Hemiargus ceraunus*) to land upon.

Even the Monarch (*Danaus plexippus*) needs to alight on a flower to feed. The big, sturdy heads of many composites can adequately bear the weight of this large butterfly.

Larval Host Plants

Following a close second only to adult nectar sources, larval host plants are key ingredients to any successful butterfly garden. They are generally not as showy, nor are they absolutely necessary to attract adult butterflies. However, a garden composed solely of nectar plants provides nothing more than a simple fast-food refueling spot. It completely ignores the requirements of the other stages of a butterfly's life cycle. Consequently, adult butterflies will come into the garden to feed but soon leave.

Larval host plants offer butterflies a reason to stay and not just pass through. Adults drawn into the garden by colorful nectar plants will now find all the necessary resources to reproduce. You will soon notice some of the same individuals returning day after day and many of the same butterfly species becoming garden regulars. Most adult butterflies tend not to wander far from their larval hosts. You may also notice a greater number of butterflies. Instead of just attracting individuals from the surrounding area, your garden will become a small butterfly factory, constantly producing new adults from the maturing larvae present.

A female Barred Sulphur (*Eurema daira*) flies toward the leaves of its host plant, Joint Vetch (*Aeschynomene americana*), to lay her eggs. Planting a variety of larval host plants will attract female butterflies into the garden.

Right: Young Hackberry Butterfly larvae (*Asterocampa celtis*) feed gregariously on sugarberry. Although caterpillars have large appetites, most can feed on a very limited variety of plant species.

Below: A fifth instar Variegated Fritillary larva (*Euptoieta claudia*) chews the leaves of Maypop (*Passiflora incarnata*).

Other Attractants

Not all butterflies are exclusively attracted to flowers. Many species, such as Red-spotted Purples, Leaf Wings, Question Marks, Tawny Emperors, Hackberry Butterflies, Mourning Cloaks, Malachites, and Buckeyes, as well as some satyrs and wood nymphs, are also drawn to or feed solely on tree sap, rotting fruit, dung, or carrion.

To accommodate their needs, simply place shallow dishes on the ground at various locations throughout the garden. Fill them with a selection of rotting fruit, banana peels, and melon rinds—the more rotten the better. Mash large pieces or whole fruit to help increase the available surface area and expose the juicy interior. Once a week or so, rinse out each dish with a garden hose and refill. If

A bowl of fruit placed in the garden helps draw in butterfly species that flowers do not attract. Papayas, mangoes, peaches, bananas, and watermelon are butterfly favorites.

Many brush-footed butterfly species might be attracted to this pine sap flow.

ants are a problem, fill a slightly larger dish with water and set the smaller fruit dish in the center. This creates a small moat and prevents the ants but not the butterflies from gaining access to the tasty meal. Finally, have patience. Don't expect the dishes to be teeming with butterflies the next day. It may take some time for them to locate the food.

Water

Males of many butterfly species commonly gather at stream banks, mud puddles, moist gravel, or damp sand for access to water, dissolved salts, and amino acids. Such groupings are typically referred to as "puddle-clubs" and can form rather impressive displays. For the more ambitious butterfly gardener, artificial mud puddles or water stations can be created with varying degrees of effort. The simplest method is to fill a large plastic container, such as a sweater storage box, with sand. Locate an open, sunlit area of your garden, dig a shallow hole, and place the container in the ground so that the rim is even with the top of the soil. Fill in any gaps around the outside of the container with loose earth and thoroughly wet the sand. The plastic container will hold in the water and keep the sand moist for some time.

The same process can be accomplished on a larger scale by lining an existing depression or newly dug hole with plastic. Make sure that the edges of the plastic are covered with soil and fill the center with sand or small gravel. A slightly concave design will facilitate moisture collection from occasional rain and regular waterings. The spray from a small garden fountain placed nearby can also help keep the ground consistently moist.

To make the area even more attractive, initially mix in a small amount of table salt with the sand or occasionally add a capful of natural fish emulsion (an organic fertilizer available at most garden centers).

Several Sleepy Orange (*Eurema nicippe*) adults gather at moist sand to imbibe salts and amino acids released into solution by the water.

Shelter

In addition to food and water, butterflies often need protection from wind, rain, temperature extremes, and predators. The easiest way to accomplish this in the garden is by including a wide variety of different plants, including shrubs and small trees. Try also to cluster vegetation and add a few nondeciduous species. Given time, as your garden grows and matures, the diversity of plantings will naturally create microclimates, or small localized environments, that offer butterflies shelter.

During periods of inclement weather and while sleeping at night, butterflies seek shelter amongst vege-tation. This Zebra Longwing (*Heliconius charitonius*) clings to the underside of a Fire Bush branch during a brief rain shower.

BUTTERFLY GARDENS FOR THREE FLORIDA CLIMATES

Florida is divided into three growing regions, or "hardiness zones." Hardiness Zone 8 is in northern Florida, north and west of a line that runs from Fernandina Beach on the Atlantic Coast to Cedar Key on the Gulf Coast. Hardiness Zone 9 is in central Florida; it runs south from Zone 8 to a line that connects Fort Pierce and Port Charlotte. Zone 10, south Florida, runs from Zone 9 down into the Florida Keys (the lower Keys are actually Zone 11). These zones are approximate, but they give a good idea of where a plant will thrive. For example, if a plant is rated for Zone 10, where there is almost no winter chill and plenty of moisture, it will have trouble in Zone 8 with its periodic freezes and relative dryness.

This section shows garden designs for each of Florida's major growing regions. Decide which hardiness zone is most appropriate for you: north Florida (Zone 8), central Florida (Zone 9), or south Florida (Zone 10). Then use our sample designs and the other charts and tables in this book to plan your garden.

The following information is highly condensed. You may want to look into some books that give more details about planning, planting, and maintaining a garden. There are two companion books in this series that can help you: *Your Florida Guide to Bedding Plants,* and *Your Florida Guide to Shrubs.*

Planning Your Garden

1. Decide where to put your butterfly garden. Our designs are planned around a lawn, but you might have a smaller area in mind that you want to fill with flowers. Perhaps you already have a dogwood or redbud, and you'd like to plan a small area around it that would attract butterflies. Take ideas from our sample designs and apply them to your yard.

2. Start a plan on paper. You can do exactly what we did. Get some graph paper and mark out the area of your yard that you'd like to convert to a butterfly garden.

3. Decide what plants you want to use and where they should go. Make notes on your yard design that indicate where you want to use each plant. Just as in the sample, draw some circles and label them; you'll begin to picture in your mind how the landscape will look when planted. Observe how much sunlight different parts of the garden area get. Is one area especially shady? Does another get sunlight all day? Examine your plan. Have you put shade plants in the sun, or sun-loving plants in the shade?

4. Check your soil. If you are planting a new garden and aren't sure how plants will grow in the area you've selected, you might want to take some time to examine your soil. Look around the area you've selected. Is the soil moist and rich or is it sandy and dry? Your local Extension office can have your soil tested. This takes a little extra time, but the more you know about your yard, the more likely you are to plan a successful garden.

5. Get some advice. Lastly, take your plan to the nursery. A professional grower can give you invaluable advice before you invest in plants.

Planting Your Garden

Planting involves more than just digging a hole and dropping a plant in the ground. When plants are removed from the pots they have been grown in, they need a well-prepared site, and they need time to "establish" in their new home.

1. Prepare a hole for the plant. Dig a generous hole. The hole should be no deeper than the plant's root ball or a little less. But the hole should be two or three times the diameter of the plant pot.

2. Carefully remove the plant from its pot. The root ball should be firm but not root bound. If you notice thick roots that grow around the root ball (because they had nowhere else to go), take shears and make three or four cuts top to bottom on the outside surface of the root ball.

3. Plant the plant. Place the plant in the center of the planting hole and ensure that it remains upright. Then replace about half the fill dirt. Tamp it gently to firm it a little and hold the plant in place, but don't pack it down. Finish filling the hole and gently tamp again. Make sure that the soil is level with the top of the root ball but no higher.

4. Before you stop: Water. You may want to place some mulch, but leave the top of the root ball exposed. Then as a finishing touch, be sure to water. Your new plant will be thirsty after all that work!

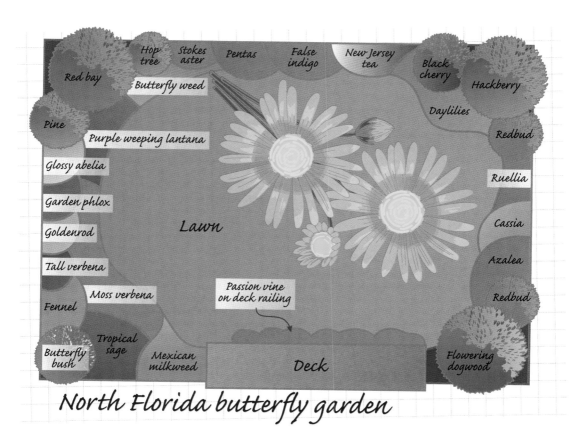

North Florida butterfly garden

Central Florida butterfly garden

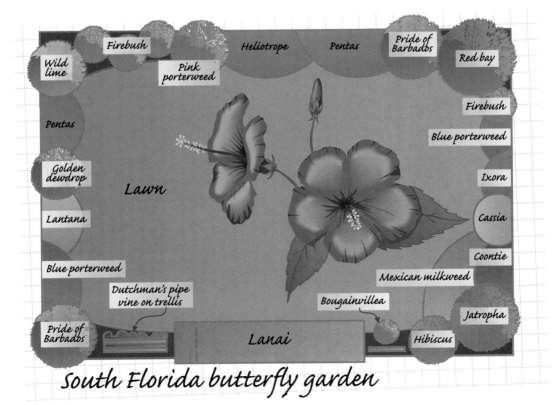

South Florida butterfly garden

Maintaining Your Butterfly Garden

The amount of maintenance a butterfly garden requires varies considerably depending on size, location, design style, the plant species included, the season, and current weather conditions. Here are a few basic tips that will help you keep your garden healthy, productive, and looking its best.

1. Give new plants a good start. Without a little help, new plants can quickly become stressed. As a result, they are more vulnerable to disease and pest attack. They may grow poorly and even die if not properly attended. Therefore, make sure to mulch and regularly water all new plants. This will help reduce weed competition, keep them from drying out, and ensure that they become firmly established. The contented plants will reward you with vigorous growth and healthy blossoms.

Mulch around new plants to help conserve moisture and reduce weed competition.

2. Fertilize regularly. Routine fertilizer applications will help produce maximum plant growth and flower production. There are many good fertilizers currently on the market. Picking the one that's right for you will depend on your garden's size and location, what plants you have, and the total amount of time and money you want to spend. Consult a local nursery specialist or Extension agent if you have questions about specific fertilizers or particular plant requirements. When using fertilizer, always read the product label first and carefully follow the directions. Excessive amounts or overuse can damage plants.

3. Avoid pesticides when possible. All butterfly life stages are extremely sensitive to pesticides. Even the slightest drift from nearby spraying can be deadly. Fortunately, there are many sound alternatives to pesticide use. One of the easiest ways to thwart pest outbreaks is to stop them before they begin.

This is best accomplished through regular garden care. Routine watering, weeding, and fertilizer application will help keep your plants healthy and stress-free. Remember, stressed or weakened plants are more susceptible to disease and pest attack. Also, periodically check your plants for pests. Large infestations always start out small. If you come across any undesirable insects, clip off and destroy the affected leaf or branch. In many cases, this is enough to control the problem.

Try using beneficial insects. Many specialty nurseries, gardening companies, and seed catalogs offer a wide selection of these natural predators. They are relatively inexpensive and fun to watch.

The only biological control to avoid at all costs is Bt. *Bacillus thuringiensis* (or Bt) is a natural bacterial disease that is harmless to adult butterflies and humans, but deadly to most larvae.

From time to time, though, pesticides need to be used. In such cases, always choose the least toxic chemical first. Insecticidal soaps, for example, can be effective against many common garden pests. They are harmless to humans and generally biodegradable. If the problem persists, move on to a stronger chemical. Only apply pesticides to the infested branch or plant—*never* treat the entire garden. Avoid using systemic pesticides on larval host plants. Unlike contact poisons, systemic pesticides are taken up by the plant. They kill when an insect eats the treated vegetation.

Consult a local nursery specialist or Extension agent if you have questions about specific pesticides or other control measures. When using chemicals, always read the product label first and carefully follow the directions.

4. Trim off old blossoms. The periodic "dead-heading," or removal of old, spent blossoms on your nectar plants, will encourage the continued production of new flowers. It can also extend the flowering period of some species. Just a little bit of effort from time to time will help your plants look better and be more prolific. The butterflies will thank you.

"Dead-heading" often extends the flowering season of many species like this Blanket Flower (*Gaillardia pulchella*) while keeping the plants looking neat.

GET STARTED TODAY! CONTAINER GARDENS FOR BUTTERFLIES

Container gardens are great projects for many reasons. You can stop by a nursery, pick up a few items, and have your first butterfly garden in an hour or two. It's a great way to start small and begin attracting butterflies. Of course, you can make more than one and create a garden layout with containers.

Container gardens are ideal for apartment dwellers, on patios, or on a balcony. They make great projects for children; this is an excellent way for little ones to learn about plants and butterflies.

The following plans are suitable for any location in Florida. As with any container plant, check them when it's hot or dry to see if they need water, and shelter them from extreme cold temperatures. Exposed container plants are more susceptible to cold temperatures than plants in the ground.

In the two illustrations that follow, we've shown specific plant selections. The illustration on the facing page, top, shows a basic selection of six plants; on the bottom, we've used some different varieties and substituted a small trellis with passionflower growing on it. You can use the plants we suggested or you can substitute any of the herbaceous perennials found in the "Quick Guide to Adult Nectar Sources" at the end of the book. Take the book with you to the nursery, and use it to plan your container garden on the spot.

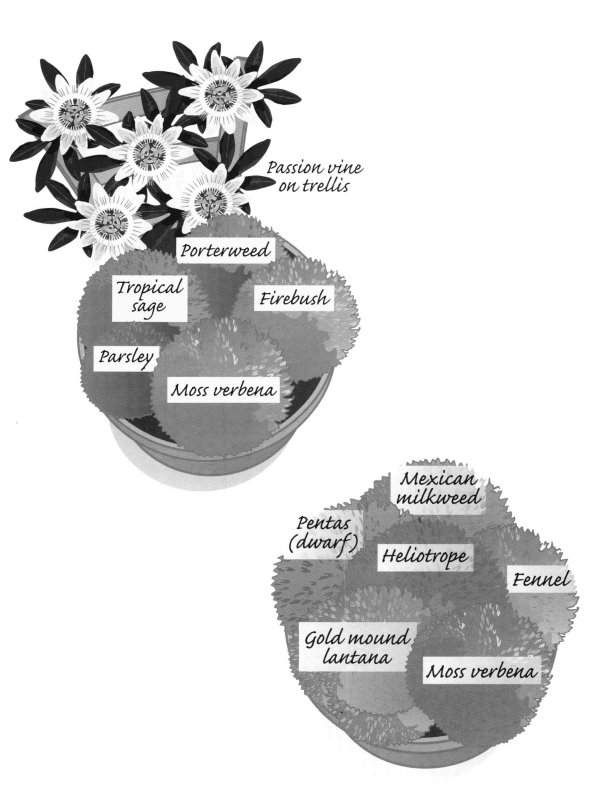

Passion vine
on trellis

Porterweed

Tropical
sage

Firebush

Parsley

Moss verbena

Mexican
milkweed

Pentas
(dwarf)

Heliotrope

Fennel

Gold mound
lantana

Moss verbena

Recipe for Small Container Garden

Selection of 4 to 6 plants (4 oz pots)
Small bag potting soil
Clay pot (or equivalent plastic pot) of suitable size

Recipe for Large Container Garden

Selection of 4 to 6 plants (1 gal pots)
Large bag potting soil
Clay pot (or equivalent plastic pot) of suitable size

Extra Large Container Garden

You can make an even larger container garden by using a half barrel and scaling up the size of the plant you purchase. Your nursery specialist can advise you about putting together this extra-large project.

General Instructions

1. Place a stone or clay shard over the drainage hole at the base of the container to prevent soil from escaping. Check to make sure that water can flow out through the hole.

2. Place enough potting soil in the container that the root ball will be within one inch of the top of the container.

3. Carefully remove the plants from their pots. (See the instructions in the "Planting Your Garden" section.)

4. Arrange the plants in the container.

5. Fill the space around the plants with potting soil and gently press everything into place. Do not pack the soil or plants tightly.

6. Water gently until you observe water coming from the bottom of the container. If your container is clay, water the outside. The clay can absorb a lot of water from the soil and make your watering less effective.

GUIDE TO COMMON FLORIDA BUTTERFLIES

The butterflies pictured in this section are grouped according to families (see "A Note about Scientific Names" in the introduction). Here's a list of all the butterflies that are pictured in the following pages:

Family Papilionidae (Swallowtail Butterflies)
Black Swallowtail (*Papilio polyxenes*)
Giant Swallowtail (*Papilio cresphontes*)
Palamedes Swallowtail (*Papilio palamedes*)
Pipevine Swallowtail (*Battus philenor*)
Polydamus Swallowtail (*Battus polydamas*)
Spicebush Swallowtail (*Papilio troilus*)
Tiger Swallowtail (*Papilio glaucus*)
Zebra Swallowtail (*Eurytides marcellus*)

Family Pieridae (Whites and Sulphurs)
Barred Sulphur (*Eurema daira*)
Cabbage Butterfly (*Pieris rapae*)
Checkered White (*Pontia protodice*)
Cloudless Sulphur (*Phoebis sennae*)
Dainty Sulphur (*Nathalis iole*)
Dogface (*Zerene cesonia*)
Great Southern White (*Ascia monuste*)
Little Yellow (*Eurema lisa*)
Orange-barred Sulphur (*Phoebis philea*)
Sleepy Orange (*Eurema nicippe*)

Family Danaidae (Milkweed Butterflies)
Monarch (*Danaus plexippus*)
Queen (*Danaus gilippus*)

Family Lycaenidae (Gossamer Wings)
Atala (*Eumaeus atala florida*)
Ceraunus Blue (*Hemiargus ceraunus*)
Gray Hairstreak (*Strymon melinus*)
Great Purple Hairstreak (*Atlides halesus*)
Red-banded Hairstreak (*Calycopis cecrops*)
Southern Hairstreak (*Fixsenia favonius*)
White M Hairstreak (*Parrhasius m-album*)

Family Libytheidae (Snout Butterflies)
Snout Butterfly (*Libytheana bachmanii*)

Family Nymphalidae (Brush-footed Butterflies)
American Painted Lady (*Vanessa virginiensis*)
Buckeye (*Junonia coenia*)
Goatweed Butterfly (*Anaea andria*)
Gulf Fritillary (*Agraulis vanillae*)
Hackberry Butterfly (*Asterocampa celtis*)
Julia (*Dryas iulia*)
Malachite (*Siproeta stelenes*)
Phaon Crescent (*Phyciodes phaon*)
Red Admiral (*Vanessa atalanta*)
Red-spotted Purple (*Limenitis arthemis astyanax*)
Tawny Emperor (*Asterocampa clyton*)
Variegated Fritillary (*Euptoieta claudia*)
Viceroy (*Limenitis archippus floridensis*)
White Peacock (*Anartia jatrophae*)
Zebra Longwing (*Heliconius charitonius*)

Family Hesperiidae (Skippers)
Checkered Skipper (*Pyrgus communis*)
Long-tailed Skipper (*Urbanus proteus*)
Silver-spotted Skipper (*Epargyreus clarus*)

Family Satyridae (Wood Nymphs and Satyrs)
Little Wood Satyr (*Megisto cymela*)

Black Swallowtail, adult female

Black Swallowtail, adult male

Family Papilionidae (Swallowtail Butterflies)

Black Swallowtail

Scientific Name: *Papilio polyxenes*
Size: 3.0 to 5.0 inches
Range: All of Florida
Flight: March to November
Habitat: Meadows, old fields, pastures, roadsides, and gardens
Larval Host Plants: Wild and cultivated members of the carrot family (*Apiaceae*) including Fennel (*Foeniculum vulgare*), Dill (*Anethum graveolens*), Parsley (*Petroselinium crispum*), Wild Carrot (*Daucus carota*), Mock Bishop's Weed (*Ptilimnium capillaceum*). Common Rue (*Ruta graveolens*) is also used.

Giant Swallowtail

Scientific Name: *Papilio cresphontes*
Size: 4.5 to 5.5 inches
Range: All of Florida
Flight: Year-round
Habitat: Open woodland, forest edges, roadsides, and orange groves
Larval Host Plants: Hercules'-club (*Zanthoxylum clava-hercules*), Wild Lime (*Zanthoxylum fagara*), Common Rue (*Ruta graveolens*), Hop Tree (*Ptelea trifoliata*), Torchwood (*Amyris elemifera*), Orange, Lemon, and Grapefruit (*Citrus* spp.)

Giant Swallowtail

Palamedes Swallowtail

Scientific Name: *Papilio palamedes*
Size: 3.5 to 5.2 inches
Range: All of Florida
Flight: February to late November
Habitat: Moist woodlands, roadsides, and pastures
Larval Host Plants: Red Bay (*Persea borbonia*), Swamp Bay (*Persea palustris*), Sweet Bay (*Magnolia virginiana*)

Pipevine Swallowtail

Scientific Name: *Battus philenor*
Size: 2.75 to 4.5 inches
Range: Entire state except southern tip and Florida Keys
Flight: February to November
Habitat: Woodlands, forest edges, roadsides, meadows, and pastures
Larval Host Plants: Pipevines (*Aristolochia* spp.) including Virginia Snakeroot (*Aristolochia serpentaria*), Dutchman's Pipe (*Aristolochia macrophylla*)

Polydamus Swallowtail

Scientific Name: *Battus polydamus*
Size: 4.0 to 5.0 inches
Range: Resident in southern portion of the state, rare in south-central, occasional elsewhere
Flight: March through November
Habitat: Old fields, meadows, and suburban gardens
Larval Host Plants: Pipevines (*Aristolochia* spp.) including *A. serpentaria, A. elegans, A. gigantea,* and *A. pentandra*

Spicebush Swallowtail

Scientific Name: *Papilio troilus*
Size: 3.5 to 5.0 inches
Range: Entire state except Florida Keys
Flight: February to late November
Habitat: Open woodland, forest edges, meadows, roadsides, and pastures
Larval Host Plants: Sassafras (*Sassafras albidum*), Spicebush (*Lindera benzoin*), Camphor Tree (*Cinnamonum camphora*), Red Bay (*Persea borbonia*), Swamp Bay (*Persea palustris*)

Tiger Swallowtail

Scientific Name: *Papilio glaucus*
Size: 3.5 to 5.5 inches
Range: Entire state except Florida Keys
Flight: February to November
Habitat: Open woodland, forest edges, roadsides, meadows, and pastures
Larval Host Plants: Black Cherry (*Prunus serotina*), Ash (*Fraxinus* spp.), Sweet Bay (*Magnolia virginiana*)

adult male

adult female, dark form

adult female, yellow form

Zebra Swallowtail

Scientific Name: *Eurytides marcellus*
Size: 2.5 to 4.0 inches
Range: All of Florida
Flight: February to December
Habitat: Open woodland, pinelands, forest edges, meadows, roadsides, and pastures
Larval Host Plants: Pawpaw (*Asimina* spp.)

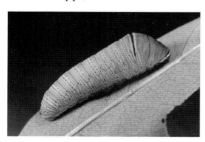

adult, summer form

adult, winter form

Family Pieridae (Whites and Sulphurs)

Barred Sulphur

Scientific Name: *Eurema daira*
Size: 1.3 to 1.8 inches
Range: All of Florida
Flight: Year-round
Habitat: Open, sunny locations such as disturbed sites, old fields, meadows, pastures, roadsides, retention ponds, moist ditches, and pinelands
Larval Host Plants: Pencil Flower (*Stylosanthes biflora, Stylosanthes hamata*), Joint Vetch (*Aeschynomene americana, Aeschynomene viscidula*)

Cabbage Butterfly

Scientific Name: *Pieris rapae*
Size: 1.5 to 2.0 inches
Range: Northern half of state
Flight: Potentially year-round
Habitat: Most open, sunny locations including disturbed sites, fields, roadsides, and agricultural land
Larval Host Plants: Most wild and cultivated crucifers including Peppergrass (*Lepidium* spp.), Mustards, Cabbage, and Broccoli

Checkered White

Scientific Name: *Pontia protodice*
Size: 1.5 to 2.0 inches
Range: All of Florida
Flight: March to October
Habitat: Open, sunny areas such as disturbed sites, old fields, road-sides, and agricultural fields
Larval Host Plants: Virginia Peppergrass (*Lepidium virginicum*)

Cloudless Sulphur

Scientific Name: *Phoebis sennae*
Size: 2.5 to 3.0 inches
Range: All of Florida
Flight: Year-round
Habitat: Open, sunny areas such as disturbed sites, old fields, mead-ows, pastures, roadsides, and agricultural fields
Larval Host Plants: Various wild and ornamental cassias including Sickle-pod Senna (*Cassia obtusifolia*), Coffee Senna (*Cassia occidentalis*), Sensitive Pea (*Cassia nictitans*), Wild Senna (*Cassia hebecarpa*), and Partridge Pea (*Cassia fasciculata*)

Dainty Sulphur

Scientific Name: *Nathalis iole*
Size: 0.75 to 1.25 inches
Range: All of Florida
Flight: Year-round, especially in southern portions of the state
Habitat: Open, sunny, and dry locations including fields, agricultural land, roadsides, and disturbed sites
Larval Host Plants: Spanish Needles (*Bides alba*) and Carpetweed (*Mollugo verticillata*)

Dogface

Scientific Name: *Zerene cesonia*
Size: 2.0 to 2.75 inches
Range: All of Florida
Flight: Year-round in southern half of state
Habitat: Open, sunny, and dry locations such as oak scrub, pinelands, open woodland, old fields, meadows, pastures, and roadsides
Larval Host Plants: False Indigo (*Amorpha fruticosa*), Summer Farewell (*Dalea pinnata*), Alfalfa (*Medicago sativa*)

Great Southern White

Scientific Name: *Ascia monuste*
Size: 1.75 to 2.5 inches
Range: Southern half of state
Flight: Year-round
Habitat: Open, sunny areas such as disturbed sites, old fields, and roadsides
Larval Host Plants: Virginia Peppergrass (*Lepidium virginicum*), Saltwort (*Batis maritima*), Limber Caper (*Capparis flexuosa*)

Little Yellow

Scientific Name: *Eurema lisa*
Size: 1.0 to 1.5 inches
Range: All of Florida
Flight: Year-round
Habitat: Most open, sunny, and dry locations including fields, pastures, roadsides, and disturbed sites
Larval Host Plants: Partridge Pea (*Cassia fasciculata*) and Sensitive Pea (*Cassia nictitans*)

Orange-barred Sulphur

Scientific Name: *Phoebis philea*
Size: 2.75 to 3.25 inches
Range: Southern portion of state, strays northward
Flight: Year-round
Habitat: Open woodlands to urban gardens
Larval Host Plants: Native and ornamental cassias (*Cassia* spp.)

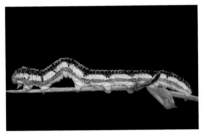

Sleepy Orange

Scientific Name: *Eurema nicippe*
Size: 1.5 to 2.25 inches
Range: All of Florida
Flight: Year-round
Habitat: Open, sunny areas such as disturbed sites, old fields, meadows, pastures, roadsides, and agricultural fields
Larval Host Plants: Various wild and ornamental cassias including Sickle-pod Senna (*Cassia obtusifolia*), Coffee Senna (*Cassia occidentalis*), Wild Senna (*Cassia hebecarpa*)

Family Danaidae
(Milkweed Butterflies)

Monarch

Scientific Name: *Danaus plexippus*
Size: 3.5 to 4.0 inches
Range: All of Florida
Flight: March to November; year-round in southernmost portion of state
Habitat: Open, sunny areas such as old fields, meadows, pastures, and roadsides
Larval Host Plants: Various milkweeds (*Asclepias* spp.), including Mexican Milkweed (*A. curassavica*), Sandhill Milkweed (*A. humistrata*), Swamp Milkweed (*A. incarnata*), and White Swamp Milkweed (*A. perennis*)

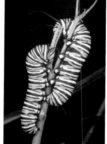

Queen

Scientific Name: *Danaus gilippus*
Size: 3.0 to 3.8 inches
Range: All of Florida
Flight: Year-round
Habitat: Open, sunny areas such as old fields, meadows, pastures, pinelands, and roadsides
Larval Host Plants: Various milkweeds (*Asclepias* spp.), including Mexican Milkweed (*A. curassavica*), Sandhill Milkweed (*A. humistrata*), Swamp Milkweed (*A. incarnata*), White Swamp Milk-weed (*A. perennis*), and Butterfly Weed (*A. tuberosa*)

Family Lycaenidae (Gossamer Wings)

Atala

Scientific Name: *Eumaeus atala florida*
Size: 1.5 to 2.0 inches
Range: Extreme south Florida
Flight: Year-round
Habitat: Tropical hardwood hammocks
Larval Host Plants: Coontie (*Zamia pumila*)

Ceraunus Blue

Scientific Name: *Hemiargus ceraunus*
Size: 0.6 to 1.2 inches
Range: All of Florida
Flight: February to December
Habitat: Open, sunny areas such as disturbed sites, old fields, pastures, and roadsides
Larval Host Plants: Various legumes particularly *Indigofera spicata*, *I. caroliniana*, and Milk-pea (*Galactia* spp.)

Gray Hairstreak

Scientific Name: *Strymon melinus*
Size: 1.0 to 1.25 inches
Range: All of Florida
Flight: February to November
Habitat: Open, sunny locations such as disturbed sites, meadows, old fields, pastures, and roadsides
Larval Host Plants: Numerous plants in many families, including clovers, vetches, sidas, tick-trefoils, and mallows

Great Purple Hairstreak

Scientific Name: *Atlides halesus*
Size: 1.25 to 2.0 inches
Range: All of Florida
Flight: Year-round
Habitat: Near forested areas
Larval Host Plants: Mistletoe (*Phoradendron serotinum*)

Red-banded Hairstreak

Scientific Name: *Calycopis cecrops*
Size: 0.75 to 1.0 inches
Range: All of Florida
Flight: Year-round
Habitat: Forest edges
Larval Host Plants: Wax Myrtle
(*Myrica cerifera*), Winged Sumac
(*Rhus copallina*)

Southern Hairstreak

Scientific Name: *Fixsenia favonius*
Size: 1.0 to 1.25 inches
Range: Most of Florida except
Panhandle
Flight: February to June
Habitat: Forest edges
Larval Host Plants: Oaks (*Quercus*
spp.), including Live Oak (*Q.*
virginiana)

White M Hairstreak

Scientific Name: *Parrhasius m-album*
Size: 1.0 to 1.5 inches
Range: All of Florida
Flight: February to November
Habitat: Forest edges
Larval Host Plants: Oaks (*Quercus* spp.), including Live Oak (*Q. virginiana*)

Family Libytheidae (Snout Butterflies)

Snout Butterfly

Scientific Name: *Libytheana bachmanii*
Size: 1.5 to 2.0 inches
Range: Entire state except Florida Keys
Flight: March to November
Habitat: Woodlands and forest edges
Larval Host Plants: Common Hackberry (*Celtis occidentalis*), Georgia Hackberry (*C. tenuifolia*), Sugarberry (*C. laevigata*)

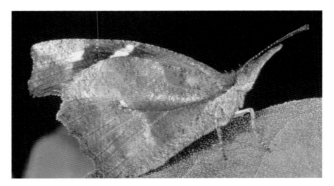

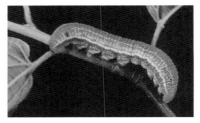

Family Nymphalidae (Brush-footed Butterflies)

American Painted Lady

Scientific Name: *Vanessa virginiensis*
Size: 1.75 to 2.5 inches
Range: All of Florida
Flight: February to December
Habitat: Open, sunny areas such as disturbed old fields, meadows, pastures, agricultural fields, and roadsides
Larval Host Plants: Cudweeds (*Gnaphalium* spp.)

Buckeye

Scientific Name: *Junonia coenia*
Size: 1.8 to 2.5 inches
Range: All of Florida
Flight: Year-round
Habitat: Open, sunny areas such as disturbed old fields, meadows, pastures, agricultural fields, and roadsides
Larval Host Plants: A wide variety of plants in many families including Plantain (*Plantago* spp.), Gerardia (*Agalinus* spp.), Toadflax (*Linaria* spp.), Wild Petunia (*Ruellia* spp.), and Twinflower (*Dyschoriste* spp.)

Goatweed Butterfly

Scientific Name: *Anaea andria*
Size: 2.0 to 2.5 inches
Range: Northern third of the state
Flight: Potentially year-round, more common in spring and summer months
Habitat: Woodlands and forest edges
Larval Host Plants: Croton (*Croton* spp.) including *C. argyranthemus*

adult, wings closed

adult, wings open

Gulf Fritillary

Scientific Name: *Agraulis vanillae*
Size: 2.5 to 3.2 inches
Range: All of Florida
Flight: Year-round in locations without a hard freeze
Habitat: Open, sunny areas such as old fields, meadows, pastures, and roadsides
Larval Host Plants: Various native and exotic passionflower vines including Maypop (*Passiflora incarnata*), Yellow Passionflower (*P. lutea*), Corky-stemmed Passionflower (*P. suberosa*), Blue Passionflower (*P. caerulea*), and Many-flowered Passionflower (*P. multiflora*)

Hackberry Butterfly

Scientific Name: *Asterocampa celtis*
Size: 2.0 to 2.5 inches
Range: All of Florida
Flight: April to November
Habitat: Woodlands and forest edges
Larval Host Plants: Common Hackberry (*Celtis occidentalis*), Georgia Hackberry (*C. tenuifolia*), Sugarberry (*C. laevigata*)

Julia

Scientific Name: *Dryas iulia*
Size: 3.0 to 3.5 inches
Range: Southern third of state
Flight: Year-round in southernmost portion of state and Florida Keys; summer months farther north
Habitat: Tropical hardwood hammocks
Larval Host Plants: Various passionflower vines including Maypop (*Passiflora incarnata*), Corky-stemmed Passionflower (*P. suberosa*), Many-flowered Passionflower (*P. multiflora*)

Malachite

Scientific Name: *Siproeta stelenes*
Size: 3.0 to 4.0 inches
Range: South Florida and the
Florida Keys
Flight: Year-round
Habitat: Shrubby disturbed sites
and along the edges of tropical
hardwood hammocks
Larval Host Plants: Green Shrimp-
plant (*Blechum brownei*)

Phaon Crescent

Scientific Name: *Phyciodes phaon*
Size: 1.0 to 1.5 inches
Range: All of Florida
Flight: March to December in
north, year-round in south
Habitat: Open, sunny, and often
moist areas such as roadsides,
pond edges, pastures, old fields,
and disturbed sites
Larval Host Plants: Frogfruit
(*Phyla nodiflora*)

Red Admiral

Scientific Name: *Vanessa atalanta*
Size: 1.75 to 2.25 inches
Range: All of Florida
Flight: Year-round
Habitat: Woodland, forest edges, pastures, and disturbed sites
Larval Host Plants: Nettles (*Urtica* spp.), Pellitory (*Parietaria* spp.), and False Nettle (*Boehmeria* spp.)

Red-spotted Purple

Scientific Name: *Limenitis arthemis astyanax*
Size: 3.0 to 3.75 inches
Range: Northern half of state
Flight: March to November
Habitat: Open woodlands and forest edges
Larval Host Plants: Black Cherry (*Prunus serotina*)

Tawny Emperor

Scientific Name: *Asterocampa clyton*
Size: 2.3 to 2.75 inches
Range: Northern half of state
Flight: March to November
Habitat: Woodlands and forest edges
Larval Host Plants: Common Hackberry (*Celtis occidentalis*), Georgia Hackberry (*C. tenuifolia*), Sugarberry (*C. laevigata*)

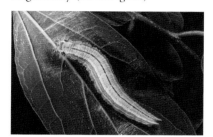

Variegated Fritillary

Scientific Name: *Euptoieta claudia*
Size: 2.0 to 2.5 inches
Range: All of Florida
Flight: February through November
Habitat: Open, sunny areas such as old fields, meadows, and pastures
Larval Host Plants: Passionflower vines including Maypop (*Passiflora incarnata*), Corky- stemmed Passionflower (*P. suberosa*), Many-flowered Passionflower (*P. multiflora*), and Violets (*Viola* spp.)

Viceroy

Scientific Name: *Limenitis archippus floridensis*
Size: 2.5 to 3.2 inches
Range: All of Florida
Flight: March to December
Habitat: Open, moist areas such as pond edges, marshes, and road-sides
Larval Host Plants: Willows (*Salix* spp.)

White Peacock

Scientific Name: *Anartia jatrophae*
Size: 2.0 to 2.8 inches
Range: Southern half of state, occasionally farther north
Flight: Year-round in south Florida
Habitat: Open, sunny, and moist areas such as roadside ditches and pond edges
Larval Host Plants: Frogfruit (*Phyla nodiflora*), Smooth Water-hyssop (*Bacopa monnieri*), Ruellia (*Ruellia occidentalis*), Green Shrimp-plant (*Blechum brownei*)

Zebra Longwing

Scientific Name: *Heliconius charitonius*
Size: 3.0 to 3.5 inches
Range: All of Florida
Flight: Year-round in locations without a hard freeze
Habitat: Woodlands and forest edges
Larval Host Plants: Various native and exotic passionflower vines including Maypop (*Passiflora incarnata*), Yellow Passionflower (*P. lutea*), Corky-stemmed Passionflower (*P. suberosa*), and Many-flowered Passionflower (*P. multiflora*)

Family Hesperiidae (Skippers)

Long-tailed Skipper

Scientific Name: *Urbanus proteus*
Size: 1.5 to 2.2 inches
Range: All of Florida
Flight: Year-round
Habitat: Open, sunny locations such as disturbed sites, old fields, meadows, agricultural fields, and roadsides
Larval Host Plants: A wide variety of legumes, including Beggar's Tick (*Desmodium* spp.) and Hog Peanut (*Amphicarpa* spp.)

Checkered Skipper

Scientific Name: *Pyrgus communis*
Size: 1.0 to 1.25 inches
Range: All of Florida
Flight: Year-round
Habitat: Open, sunny locations, including fields, disturbed sites, pastures, and roadsides
Larval Host Plants: Sidas, including *Sida rhombifolia* and *S. acuta*

Silver-spotted Skipper

Scientific Name: *Epargyreus clarus*
Size: 1.5 to 2.5 inches
Range: Northern half of Florida
Flight: February to November
Habitat: Disturbed sites to open woodland
Larval Host Plants: Various legumes, including Wisteria (*Wisteria* spp.), Beggar's Tick (*Desmodium* spp.), Indigo Bush (*Amorpha fruticosa*), Ground Nut (*Apios americana*), and Hog Peanut (*Amphicarpa* spp.)

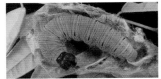

Family Satyridae (Wood Nymphs and Satyrs)

Little Wood Satyr

Scientific Name: *Megisto cymela*
Size: 1.2 to 1.7 inches
Range: Northern half of state
Flight: Late March to October
Habitat: Woodlands and forest edges
Larval Host Plants: Various grasses including St. Augustine grass (*Stenotaphrum* spp.), and Centipede grass (*Eremochloa ophiuroides*)

ADULT NECTAR SOURCES

The plants shown on the following pages are excellent sources of food for adult butterflies.

Butterfly Bush

Scientific Name: *Buddleia davidii*
Description: Weeping shrub; cultivar
Height: To 12 feet
Flower Color: Variable
Light Requirement: Full sun
Bloom Period: Year-round in south, spring to frost in north
Availability: Nurseries; most retail garden centers
Comments: Best if pruned back before spring

Dotted Horsemint

Scientific Name: *Monarda punctata*
Description: Perennial; native
Height: 1.5 to 3.0 feet
Flower Color: Cream to pink
Light Requirement: Full sun
Bloom Period: Summer to fall
Availability: Specialty and native plant nurseries
Comments: Occasional wildflower of disturbed sites; drought tolerant

Drummond Phlox

Scientific Name: *Phlox drummondii*
Description: Annual; naturalized
Height: 1.0 to 2.5 feet
Flower Color: White, pink, red
Light Requirement: Sun
Bloom Period: Spring to early summer
Availability: Many specialty and native plant nurseries; commonly available as seed
Comments: Good species for naturalizing; readily self-sows

Fire Bush

Scientific Name: *Hamelia patens*
Description: Shrub to small tree; native
Height: To 12 feet
Flower Color: Orange
Light Requirement: Partial shade to sun
Bloom Period: Year-round in south, spring to frost in north
Availability: Nurseries; many retail garden centers
Comments: Tender plant; requires protection from freezing temperatures; very drought tolerant

Fire Spike

Scientific Name: *Odontonema strictum*
Description: Perennial; non-native
Height: 2.5 to 5 feet
Flower Color: Red
Light Requirement: Shade to partial sun
Bloom Period: Late summer to frost
Availability: Nurseries; many retail garden centers
Comments: Handsome plant for shady areas

Garden Phlox

Scientific Name: *Phlox paniculata*
Description: Perennial; native, cultivar
Height: 2.5 to 5.0 feet
Flower Color: Variable
Light Requirement: Full sun
Bloom Period: Summer to mid-fall
Availability: Nurseries; many retail garden centers
Comments: Plants prefer rich soil and regular moisture

Glossy Abelia

Scientific Name: *Abelia {x} grandiflora*
Description: Weeping shrub; cultivar
Height: To 8 feet
Flower Color: Pinkish white
Light Requirement: Partial shade to full sun
Bloom Period: Late spring to November
Availability: Nurseries; many retail garden centers
Comments: Extremely vigorous grower; easily shaped with pruning

Golden Dewdrop

Scientific Name: *Duranta repens*
Description: Shrub; non-native
Height: To 15 feet
Flower Color: Blue, white
Light Requirement: Sun
Bloom Period: February to November
Availability: Nurseries; most retail garden centers
Comments: Easily shaped with pruning; requires regular moisture for best display

Indian Blanket

Scientific Name: *Gaillardia pulchella*
Description: Annual; native
Height: 1.0 to 2.0 feet
Flower Color: Red and yellow
Light Requirement: Sun
Bloom Period: Spring to frost
Availability: Nurseries; many retail garden centers
Comments: Common roadside wildflower; good for naturalizing

Joe-pye Weed

Scientific Name: *Eupatorium fistulosum*
Description: Perennial; native, cultivar
Height: 3.5 to 9.0 feet
Flower Color: Pink
Light Requirement: Part shade to full sun
Bloom Period: Late summer to October
Availability: Many specialty and native plant nurseries
Comments: Plants prefer rich soils and regular moisture

Mexican Heather

Scientific Name: *Cuphea hysoppifolia*
Description: Perennial; non-native
Height: 1.0 to 2.5 feet
Flower Color: Various
Light Requirement: Sun
Bloom Period: Year-round in south; spring to frost in north
Availability: Nurseries; most retail garden centers
Comments: Especially attractive to skippers

Mexican Milkweed

Scientific Name: *Asclepias curassavica*
Description: Perennial; non-native
Height: 1.5 to 3 feet
Flower Color: Yellow-orange
Light Requirement: Full sun
Bloom Period: Year-round in south, spring to frost in north
Availability: Nurseries; most retail garden centers
Comments: Both adult nectar source and larval host plant; easily started from seed

Mexican Petunia

Scientific Name: *Ruellia brittoniana*
Description: Perennial; cultivar
Height: 2.5 to 4.0 feet
Flower Color: Blue/purple
Light Requirement: Sun
Bloom Period: Spring through fall
Availability: Nurseries; most retail garden centers
Comments: Provides better show if cut back before spring

Mexican Sage

Scientific Name: *Salvia leucantha*
Description: Perennial; non-native
Height: To 4.5 feet
Flower Color: Bluish lavender
Light Requirement: Full sun
Bloom Period: Summer to December
Availability: Nurseries; many retail garden centers
Comments: Plants can be pruned back during the growing season to maintain a manageable size

Moss Verbena

Scientific Name: *Glandularia pulchella*
Description: Low, spreading perennial; non-native
Height: To 1.0 foot
Flower Color: Various
Light Requirement: Sun
Bloom Period: Year-round
Availability: Nurseries; many retail garden centers
Comments: Common wildflower of disturbed sites; good ground cover

New Jersey Tea

Scientific Name: *Ceanothus americanus*
Description: Shrub; native
Height: 1.0 to 3.5 feet
Flower Color: White
Light Requirement: Sun
Bloom Period: Spring to early summer
Availability: Specialty and native plant nurseries
Comments: Frequent shrub of dry, open areas; drought tolerant

Pentas

Scientific Name: *Pentas lanceolata*
Description: Perennial; non-native
Height: 1 to 3 feet
Flower Color: white, pink, lavender, red (red recommended)
Light Requirement: Full sun
Bloom Period: Year-round in south, spring to frost in north
Availability: Nurseries, most retail garden centers
Comments: Tender perennial; requires protection from freezing temperatures

Porter Weed

Scientific Name: *Stachytarphaeta urticifolia*
Description: Perennial; native, cultivar
Height: 2.5 to 5 feet
Flower Color: Various
Light Requirement: Prefers full sun
Bloom Period: Year-round in south, spring to frost in north
Availability: Nurseries; many retail garden centers
Comments: Tender perennial; requires protection from freezing temperatures

Purple Weeping Lantana

Scientific Name: *Lantana montevidensis*
Description: Weeping shrub; non-native
Height: Variable, can reach several feet if not pruned back
Flower Color: Pink/lavender
Light Requirement: Full sun
Bloom Period: Year-round in south, spring to frost in north
Availability: Nurseries; most retail garden centers
Comments: Allow plenty of room for plants to grow; spreads readily; drought tolerant

Redbud

Scientific Name: *Cercis canadensis*
Description: Small tree; native
Height: To 30 feet
Flower Color: Pink
Light Requirement: Partial shade to full sun
Bloom Period: Spring
Availability: Nurseries; most retail garden centers
Comments: Extremely ornamental; good spring nectar source for many small butterfly species

Stokes' Aster

Scientific Name: *Stokesia laevis*
Description: Perennial; native, numerous cultivars
Height: 1 to 2 feet
Flower Color: Blue
Light Requirements: Part shade to full sun
Bloom Period: Spring through fall
Availability: Nurseries; most retail garden centers
Comments: Large, showy blooms; thrives with regular watering

Tall Verbena

Scientific Name: *Verbena bonariensis*
Description: Perennial
Height: To 6 feet
Flower Color: Lavender
Light Requirement: Full sun
Bloom Period: Spring to frost
Availability: Many nurseries
Comments: Plants can be pruned back during the growing season to maintain a manageable size

Tropical Sage

Scientific Name: *Salvia coccinea*
Description: Perennial; native
Height: 1.5 to 3.0 feet
Flower Color: Red
Light Requirements: Full sun
Bloom Period: Year-round in south, spring to frost in north
Availability: Nurseries; many retail garden centers
Comments: Adds brilliant color to the garden

Yaupon Holly

Scientific Name: *Ilex vomitoria*
Description: Shrub or small tree; native
Height: To 25 feet
Flower Color: White
Light Requirement: Part shade to full sun
Bloom Period: Spring
Availability: Nurseries; most retail garden centers
Comments: Attractive small leaves and branching habit; drought tolerant

LARVAL HOST PLANTS

The plants shown on the following pages are excellent sources of food for butterfly larvae. Plants marked with an asterisk are native Florida plants.

Black Cherry*

Scientific Name: *Prunus serotina*
Description: Tree
Height: To 90 feet
Light Requirement: Sun to partial shade
Availability: Specialty and native plant nurseries
Used By: Red-spotted Purple, Tiger Swallowtail
Comments: Rapid grower; glossy leaves and attractive white spring flowers

Calico Flower

Scientific Name: *Aristolochia elegans*
Description: Vine
Height: Variable
Light Requirement: Sun to partial shade
Availability: Specialty nurseries, some retail garden centers
Used By: Polydamus Swallowtail
Comments: Vigorous grower, unique pipe-shaped flowers

Fall Senna

Scientific Name: *Cassia bicapsularis*
Description: Shrub
Height: To 12 feet
Light Requirement: Sun
Availability: Nurseries; most retail garden centers
Used By: Orange-barred Sulphur, Cloudless Sulphur
Comments: Attractive yellow blossoms

False Indigo*

Scientific Name: *Amorpha fruticosa*
Description: Shrub
Height: To 12 feet
Light Requirement: Sun
Availability: Specialty and native plant nurseries
Used By: Dogface Butterfly, Silver-spotted Skipper
Comments: Prefers moisture; attractive, purple flowers

Fennel

Scientific Name: *Foeniculum vulgare*
Description: Perennial
Height: 15 to 40 inches
Light Requirement: Sun
Availability: Nurseries; most retail garden centers
Used By: Black Swallowtail
Comments: Attractive, aromatic foliage; culinary uses

Frogfruit*

Scientific Name: *Lippia nodiflora*
Description: Annual/perennial
Height: Less than six inches
Light Requirement: Sun
Availability: Not commercially available
Used By: Phaon Crescent, Buckeye, White Peacock
Comments: Common plant of moist, disturbed sites; creeping habit

Hercules'-club*

Scientific Name: *Zanthoxylum clava-hercules*
Description: Shrub to small tree
Height: To 30 feet
Light Requirement: Sun to partial shade
Availability: Specialty and native plant nurseries
Used By: Giant Swallowtail
Comments: Sharp spines

Maypop*

Scientific Name: *Passiflora incarnata*
Description: Perennial vine
Height: Variable
Light Requirement: Sun to shade
Availability: Nurseries; most retail garden centers
Used By: Gulf Fritillary, Zebra Longwing, Variegated Fritillary, Julia
Comments: Planting in both sun and shade will help attract different butterfly species

Partridge Pea*

Scientific Name: *Cassia fasciculata*
Description: Annual
Height: To 3 feet
Light Requirement: Sun to partial shade
Availability: Specialty and native plant nurseries
Used By: Cloudless Sulphur, Little Yellow, Gray Hairstreak
Comments: Common weedy plant of open, sunny, and disturbed sites

Pawpaw*

Scientific Name: *Asimina angustifolia*
Description: Shrub
Height: To 3 feet
Light Requirement: Sun to partial shade
Availability: Occasional availability at specialty and native plant nurseries
Used By: Zebra Swallowtail
Comments: Common plant of pine flatwoods, pastures, and old fields

Red Bay*

Scientific Name: *Persea borbonia*
Description: Large shrub or tree
Height: To 30 feet
Light Requirement: Sun to shade
Availability: Specialty and native plant nurseries
Used By: Palamedes Swallowtail, Spicebush Swallowtail
Comments: Prefers moisture; evergreen, aromatic foliage

Sassafras*

Scientific Name: *Sassafras albidum*
Description: Small tree
Height: To 20 feet
Light Requirement: Sun to partial shade
Availability: Specialty and native plant nurseries
Used By: Spicebush Swallowtail
Comments: Drought tolerant; aromatic foliage

Silver Croton*

Scientific Name: *Croton argyranthemus*
Description: Woody plant
Height: 12 to 25 inches
Light Requirement: Sun to partial shade
Availability: Specialty and native plant nurseries
Used By: Goatweed Butterfly
Comments: Attractive silvery foliage; small white flowers

Spanish Needles

Scientific Name: *Bidens alba*
Description: Annual
Height: To 36 inches
Light Requirement: Sun to partial shade
Availability: Not commercially available
Used By: Dainty Sulphur
Comments: Dead-head old blossoms to prevent seed set of this weedy plant; also good nectar source

Sugarberry*

Scientific Name: *Celtis laevigata*
Description: Tree
Height: To 60 feet
Light Requirement: Sun to shade
Availability: Specialty and native plant nurseries, some retail garden centers
Used By: Hackberry Butterfly, Tawny Emperor, Snout Butterfly, Question Mark
Comments: Attractive tree underutilized in landscapes

Sweet Bay*

Scientific Name: *Magnolia virginiana*
Description: Small tree
Height: To 25 feet
Light Requirement: Sun to partial shade
Availability: Specialty and native plant nurseries
Used By: Tiger Swallowtail
Comments: Prefers moisture; large, white flowers

Virginia Peppergrass

Scientific Name: *Lepidium virginicum*
Description: Annual
Height: 12 to 24 inches
Light Requirement: Sun
Availability: Not commercially available
Used By: Checkered White, Great Southern White, Cabbage White
Comments: Very common weed of open, sunny, and disturbed sites

Virginia Snakeroot*

Scientific Name: *Aristolochia virginiana*
Description: Perennial
Height: To 12 inches
Light Requirement: Sun to full shade
Availability: Specialty and native plant nurseries
Used By: Pipevine Swallowtail, Polydamus Swallowtail
Comments: Requires a large number of plants to feed even a few larvae

Wax Myrtle*

Scientific Name: *Myrica cerifera*
Description: Bushy shrub
Height: To 15 feet
Light Requirement: Sun to partial shade
Availability: Nurseries; most retail garden centers
Used By: Red-banded Hairstreak
Comments: Good landscape plant; aromatic leaves

White Swamp Milkweed*

Scientific Name: *Asclepias perennis*
Description: Perennial
Height: 12 to 20 inches
Light Requirement: Sun
Availability: Specialty and native plant nurseries, some retail garden centers
Used By: Monarch, Queen
Comments: Attractive white flowers, also good nectar source

Wild Lime*

Scientific Name: *Zanthoxylum fagara*
Description: Shrub or small tree
Height: To 20 feet
Light Requirement: Sun to partial shade
Availability: Specialty and native plant nurseries
Used By: Giant Swallowtail
Comments: Rapid grower and drought tolerant; sharp spines

Quick Guide to Florida Butterflies

The symbol "❧" indicates that a photograph of this butterfly or plant may be found in this book.

Butterfly	Plants Preferred by Butterfly Larvae
American Painted Lady (*Vanessa virginiensis*) ❧	Cudweeds (*Gnaphalium* spp.)
Atala (*Eumaeus atala florida*) ❧	Coontie (*Zamia pumila*)
Barred Sulphur (*Eurema daira*) ❧	Pencil Flower (*Stylosanthes biflora, S. hamata*) Joint Vetch (*Aeschynomene americana, A. viscidula*)
Black Swallowtail (*Papilio polyxenes*) ❧	Wild and cultivated members of the carrot family (*Apiaceae*), including: Fennel (*Foeniculum vulgare*) ❧ Dill (*Anethum graveolens*) Parsley (*Petroselinium crispum*) Wild Carrot (*Daucus carota*) Mock Bishop's Weed (*Ptilimnium capillaceum*). Common Rue (*Ruta graveolens*) is also used.
Buckeye (*Junonia coenia*) ❧	Plants in many families, including: Plantain (*Plantago* spp.) Gerardia (*Agalinus* spp.) Toadflax (*Linaria* spp.) Wild petunia (*Ruellia* spp.) Twinflower (*Dyschoriste* spp.)
Cabbage Butterfly (*Pieris rapae*) ❧	Most wild and cultivated crucifers, including: Peppergrass (*Lepidium* spp.) Mustards, Cabbage, and Broccoli
Ceraunus Blue (*Hemiargus ceraunus*) ❧	Various legumes, particularly: *Indigofera spicata* and *I. caroliniana* Milk-pea (*Galactia* spp.)
Checkered Skipper (*Pyrgus communis*) ❧	Sidas including *Sida rhombifolia* and *S. acuta*
Checkered White (*Pontia protodice*) ❧	Virginia Peppergrass (*Lepidium virginicum*) ❧

Cloudless Sulphur (*Phoebis sennae*) ✤	Various wild and ornamental cassias, including: Sickle-pod Senna (*Cassia obtusifolia*) Coffee Senna (*C. occidentalis*) Sensitive Pea (*C. nictitans*) Wild Senna (*C. hebecarpa*) Partridge Pea (*C. fasciculata*) ✤
Dainty Sulphur (*Nathalis iole*) ✤	Spanish Needles (*Bides alba*) ✤ Carpetweed (*Mollugo verticillata*)
Dogface (*Zerene cesonia*) ✤	False Indigo (*Amorpha fruticosa*) ✤ Summer Farewell (*Dalea pinnata*) Alfalfa (*Medicago sativa*)
Giant Swallowtail (*Papilio cresphontes*) ✤	Hercules'-club (*Zanthoxylum clava-hercules*) ✤ Wild Lime (*Zanthoxylum fagara*) ✤ Common Rue (*Ruta graveolens*) Hop Tree (*Ptelea trifoliata*) Torchwood (*Amyris elemifera*) Orange, Lemon, and Grapefruit (*Citrus* spp.)
Goatweed Butterfly (*Anaea andria*) ✤	Croton (*Croton* spp.) including *C. argyranthemus*
Gray Hairstreak (*Strymon melinus*) ✤	Numerous plants in many families, including: Clovers, Vetches, Sidas, Tick-trefoils, and Mallows
Great Purple Hairstreak (*Atlides halesus*) ✤	Mistletoe (*Phoradendron* sp.)
Great Southern White (*Ascia monuste*) ✤	Virginia Peppergrass (*Lepidium virginicum*) ✤ Saltwort (*Batis maritima*) Limber Caper (*Capparis flexuosa*)
Gulf Fritillary (*Agraulis vanillae*) ✤	Various native and exotic passionflower vines, including: Maypop (*Passiflora incarnata*) ✤ Yellow Passionflower (*Passiflora lutea*) Corky-stemmed Passionflower (*Passiflora suberosa*) Many-flowered Passionflower (*Passiflora multiflora*)
Hackberry Butterfly (*Asterocampa celtis*) ✤	Common Hackberry (*Celtis occidentalis*) Georgia Hackberry (*Celtis tenuifolia*) Sugarberry (*Celtis laevigata*) ✤

Butterfly	Plants Preferred by Butterfly Larvae
Julia (*Dryas iulia*) ✺	Various passionflower vines, including: Maypop (*Passiflora incarnata*) ✺ Corky-stemmed Passionflower (*P. suberosa*) Many-flowered Passionflower (*P. multiflora*)
Little Wood Satyr (*Megisto cymela*) ✺	Various grasses, including: St. Augustine grass (*Stenotaphrum* spp.) Centipede grass (*Eremochloa ophiuroides*)
Little Yellow (*Eurema lisa*) ✺	Partridge Pea (*Cassia fasciculata*) ✺ Sensitive Pea (*Cassia nictitans*)
Long-tailed Skipper (*Urbanus proteus*) ✺	A wide variety of legumes, including: Beggar's Tick (*Desmodium* spp.) Hog Peanut (*Amphicarpa* spp.)
Malachite (*Siproeta stelenes*) ✺	Green Shrimp-plant (*Blechum brownei*)
Monarch (*Danaus plexippus*) ✺	Various milkweeds (*Asclepias* spp.), including: Mexican Milkweed (*A. curassavica*) ✺ Sandhill Milkweed (*A. humistrata*) Swamp Milkweed (*A. incarnata*) White Swamp Milkweed (*A. perennis*) ✺
Orange-barred Sulphur (*Phoebis philea*) ✺	Native and ornamental cassias (*Cassia* spp.)
Palamedes Swallowtail (*Papilio palamedes*) ✺	Red Bay (*Persea borbonia*) ✺ Swamp Bay (*Persea palustris*) Sweet Bay (*Magnolia virginiana*) ✺
Phaon Crescent (*Phyciodes phaon*) ✺	Frogfruit (*Phyla nodiflora*) ✺
Pipevine Swallowtail (*Battus philenor*) ✺	Pipevines (*Aristolochia* spp.) including: Virginia Snakeroot (*Aristolochia serpentaria*) ✺ Dutchman's Pipe (*Aristolochia macrophylla*)
Polydamus Swallowtail (*Battus polydamus*) ✺	Pipevines (*Aristolochia* spp.) including: *A. serpentaria, A. elegans, A. gigantea,* and *A. trilobata*
Queen (*Danaus gilippus*) ✺	Various milkweeds (*Asclepias* spp.), including: Mexican Milkweed (*A. curassavica*) ✺ Sandhill Milkweed (*A. humistrata*) Swamp Milkweed (*A. incarnata*) White Swamp Milkweed (*A. perennis*) ✺ Butterfly Weed (*A. tuberosa*)

Red Admiral (*Vanessa atalanta*) ✎

Nettles (*Urtica* spp.)
Pellitory (*Parietaria* spp.)
False Nettle (*Boehmeria* spp.)

Red-banded Hairstreak (*Calycopis cecrops*) ✎

Wax Myrtle (*Myrica cerifera*) ✎
Winged Sumac (*Rhus copallina*)

Red-spotted Purple (*Limenitis arthemis astyanax*) ✎

Black Cherry (*Prunus serotina*) ✎

Silver-spotted Skipper (*Epargyreus clarus*) ✎

Various legumes, including:
Wisteria (*Wisteria* spp.)
Beggar's Tick (*Desmodium* spp.)
Indigo Bush (*Amorpha fruticosa*)
Ground Nut (*Apios americana*)
Hog Peanut (*Amphicarpa* spp.)

Sleepy Orange (*Eurema nicippe*) ✎

Various wild and ornamental cassias,
including:
Sickle-pod Senna (*Cassia obtusifolia*)
Coffee Senna (*Cassia occidentalis*)
Wild Senna (*Cassia hebecarpa*)

Snout Butterfly (*Libytheana bachmanii*) ✎

Common Hackberry (*Celtis occidentalis*)
Georgia Hackberry (*Celtis tenuifolia*)
Sugarberry (*Celtis laevigata*) ✎

Southern Hairstreak (*Fixsenia favonius*) ✎

Oaks (*Quercus* spp.), including:
Live Oak (*Quercus virginiana*)

Spicebush Swallowtail (*Papilio troilus*) ✎

Sassafras (*Sassafras albidum*) ✎
Spicebush (*Lindera benzoin*)
Camphor Tree (*Cinnamonum camphora*)
Red Bay (*Persea borbonia*) ✎
Swamp Bay (*Persea palustris*)

Tawny Emperor (*Asterocampa clyton*) ✎

Common Hackberry (*Celtis occidentalis*)
Georgia Hackberry (*Celtis tenuifolia*)
Sugarberry (*Celtis laevigata*) ✎

Tiger Swallowtail (*Papilio glaucus*) ✎

Black Cherry (*Prunus serotina*) ✎
Ash (*Fraxinus* spp.)
Sweet Bay (*Magnolia virginiana*) ✎

Variegated Fritillary (*Euptoieta claudia*) ✎

Passionflower vines, including:
Maypop (*Passiflora incarnata*) ✎
Corky-stemmed Passionflower (*P. suberosa*)
Many-flowered Passionflower
(*Passiflora multiflora*)
Violets (*Viola* spp.)

Butterfly	Plants Preferred by Butterfly Larvae
Viceroy (*Limenitis archippus floridensis*) ❧	Willows (*Salix* spp.)
White M Hairstreak (*Parrhasius m-album*) ❧	Oaks (*Quercus* spp.), including: Live Oak (*Quercus virginiana*)
White Peacock (*Anartia jatrophae*) ❧	Frogfruit (*Phyla nodiflora*) ❧ Smooth Water-hyssop (*Bacopa monnieri*) Ruellia (*Ruellia occidentalis*) Green Shrimp-plant (*Blechum brownei*)
Zebra Longwing (*Heliconius charitonius*) ❧	Various native and exotic passionflower vines, including: Maypop (*Passiflora incarnata*) ❧ Yellow Passionflower (*Passiflora lutea*) Corky-stemmed Passionflower (*Passiflora suberosa*) Many-flowered Passionflower (*Passiflora multiflora*)
Zebra Swallowtail (*Eurytides marcellus*) ❧	Pawpaw (*Asimina* spp.) ❧

Quick Guide to Adult Nectar Sources
(Grouped by Plant Type)

Trees

American Plum (*Prunus americana*)
Black Cherry (*Prunus serotina*)
Chaste Tree (*Vitex agnus-castus*)
Chickasaw Plum (*Prunus angustifolia*)
Coastal Plains Willow (*Salix caroliniana*)
Flowering Dogwood (*Cornus florida*)
Hop Tree (*Ptelea trifoliata*)
Mimosa (*Albiza julibrissum*)
Redbud (*Cercis canadensis*)

Shrubs

Azalea (*Rhododendron* sp.)
Blackberry (*Rubus* sp.)
Butterfly Bush (*Buddleia davidii*)
Button Bush (*Cephalanthus occidentalis*)
Chinese Privet (*Ligustrum sinense*)
Fire Bush (*Hamelia patens*)
Glossy Abelia (*Abelia* x *grandiflora*)
Golden Dewdrop (*Duranta repens*)
Hibiscus (*Hibiscus* sp.)
Ixora (*Ixora* sp.)
Jatropha (*Jatropha integerrima*)
New Jersey Tea (*Ceonothus americanus*)
Plumbago (*Plumbago capensis*)
Pride of Barbados (*Caeselpina pulcherima*)
Red Buckeye (*Aesculus pavia*)
Sweet Pepperbush (*Clethra alnifolia*)
Virginia Willow (*Itea virginica*)

Vines

Bougainvillea (*Bougainvillea* sp.)
Coral Vine (*Antigon leptopus*)
Honeysuckle (*Lonicera* spp.)
Mexican Flame Vine (*Senicio confusus*)
Morning Glory (*Ipomoea* spp.)
Star Jasmine (*Trachelospermum jasminoides*)

Herbaceous Perennials

Aster (*Aster* spp.)
Bachelor Button (*Centaurea* sp.)
Black-eyed Susan (*Rudbeckia hirta*)
Blazing Star (*Liatris* spp.)
Blue Sage (*Salvia azurea*)
Blue-eyed Grass (*Sisyrinchium* sp.)
Bluebeard (*Caryopteris chandonensis*)
Butterfly Weed (*Asclepias tuberosa*)
Cardinal Flower (*Lobelia cardinalis*)
Catchfly (*Silene* spp.)
Cigar Plant (*Cuphea micropetela*)
Coral Vine (*Antigon leptopus*)
Coralbean (*Erythrina heracea*)
Daylily (*Hemerocallis* sp.)
Deer Tongue (*Carphephorus* sp.)
Fire Spike (*Odontonema strictum*)
Firecracker Plant (*Russelia equisetiformis*)
Frogfruit (*Phyla nodiflora*)
Garden Phlox (*Phlox paniculata*)
Glorybower (*Clerodendrum bungei*)
Goldenaster (*Chrysopsis* sp.)
Goldenrod (*Solidago* sp.)
Groundsel (*Senecio* spp.)
Heliotrope (*Heliotropium arborescens*)
Indian Blacket (*Gaillardia pulchella*)
Indigo Bush (*Amorpha fruticosa*)
Ironweed (*Vernonia* spp.)
Joe-pye Weed (*Eupatorium fistulosum*)
Jupiter's Beard (*Centrantus ruber*)
Lantana (*Lantana* sp.)
Mexican Heather (*Cuphea hysoppifolia*)
Mexican Milkweed (*Asclepias curassavica*)
Mist Flower (*Eupatorium coelestinum*)
Moss Verbena (*Verbena tenuisecta*)
Mountain Mint (*Pycnanthemum* sp.)

Obedient Plant (*Physostegia virginiana*)
Pentas (*Pentas lanceolata*)
Porter Weed (*Stachytarphaeta urticifolia*)
Purple Coneflower (*Echinacea purpurea*)
Rattlesnake Master (*Eryngium yuccifolium*)
Sandhill Milkweed (*Asclepias humistrata*)
Sedum (*Sedum* spp.)
Shepherd's Needle (*Bidens* alba)
Shrimp-plant (*Beloperone guttata*)
Society Garlic (*Tulbaghia violacea*)
Spotted Beebalm (*Monarda punctata*)
Stokes' Aster (*Aster laevis*)
Sunflower (*Helianthus* sp.)
Swamp Milkweed (*Asclepias incarnata*)
Tall Wild Verbena (*Verbena brasiliensis*)
Tropical Sage (*Salvia coccinea*)
Tuber Vervain (*Verbena rigida*)
Verbena (*Verbena* sp.)
Wild Petunia (*Ruellia brittoniana*)
Yarrow (*Achillea millefolium*)

Quick Guide to Larval Host Plants

Plant Species	Butterfly Larvae That Use This Plant
Beggar's Tick (*Desmodium* sp.)	Long-tailed Skipper (*Urbanus proteus*)
Black Cherry (*Prunus serotina*)	Tiger Swallowtail (*Papilio glaucus*) Red-spotted Purple (*Limenitis arthemis astyanax*)
Blue Passionflower (*Passiflora caerulea*)	Gulf Fritillary (*Agraulis vanillae*)
Camphor Tree (*Cinnamonum camphora*)	Spicebush Swallowtail (*Papilio troilus*)
Cassia (*Cassia* sp.)	Cloudless Sulphur (*Phoebis sennae*) Orange-barred Sulphur (*Phoebis philea*) Sleepy Orange (*Eurema nicippe*)
Coastal Plain Willow (*Salix caroliniana*)	Viceroy (*Limenitis archippus floridensis*)
Coontie (*Zamia pumila*)	Atala (*Eumaeus atala florida*)
Corky-stemmed Passion-vine (*P. suberosa*)	Gulf Fritillary (*Agraulis vanillae*) Zebra longwing (*Heliconius charitonius*) Julia (*Dryas iulia*)
Cudweed (*Gnaphalium* sp.)	American Painted Lady (*Vanessa virginiensis*)
Dill (*Anethum graveolens*)	Black Swallowtail (*Papilio polyxenes*)
Dutchman's Pipe (*Aristolochia* sp.)	Polydamus Swallowtail (*Battus polydamus*) Pipevine Swallowtail (*Battus philenor*)
False Nettle (*Boehmeria* sp.)	Red Admiral (*Vanessa atalanta*)
False Indigo (*Amorpha fruticosa*)	Dogface Butterfly (*Zerene cesonia*)
Fennel (*Feoniculum vulgare*)	Black Swallowtail (*Papilio polyxenes*)
Frogfruit (*Phyla nodiflora*)	White Peacock (*Anartia jatrophae*) Phaon Crescent (*Pyciodes phaon*)
Gerardia (*Agalinus* sp.)	Buckeye (*Junonia coenia*)
Green Ash (*Fraxinus pennsylvanica*)	Tiger Swallowtail (*Papilio glaucus*)
Green Shrimp-plant (*Blechum brownei*)	Malachite (*Siproeta stelenes*) White Peacock (*Anartia jatrophae*)
Hercules'-club (*Zanthoxylum clava-hercules*)	Giant Swallowtail (*Papilio cresphontes*)

Hop Tree (*Ptelea trifoliata*)	Giant Swallowtail (*Papilio cresphontes*)
Indigo Bush (*Indigofera* sp.)	Ceraunus Blue (*Hemiargus ceraunus*)
Joint Vetch (*Aeschynemone* sp.)	Barred Sulphur (*Eurema daira*)
Live Oak (*Quercus virginiana*)	White M Hairstreak (*Parrhasius m-album*)
Maypop (*Passiflora incarnata*)	Zebra Longwing (*Heliconius charitonius*)
	Gulf Fritillary (*Agraulis vanillae*)
	Julia (*Dryas iulia*)
	Variegated Fritillary (*Euptoieta claudia*)
Mexican Milkweed (*Asclepias curassavica*)	Monarch (*Danaus plexippus*)
	Queen (*Danuas gilippus*)
Parsley (*Petroselinium crispum*)	Black Swallowtail (*Papilio polyxenes*)
Partridge Pea (*Cassia fasciculata*)	Cloudless Sulphur (*Phoebis sennae*)
	Little Sulphur (*Eurema lisa*)
Pawpaw (*Asimina* sp.)	Zebra Swallowtail (*Eurytides marcellus*)
Pencil Flower (*Stylosanthes biflora*)	Barred Sulphur (*Eurema daira*)
Plantain (*Plantago* sp.)	Buckeye (*Junonia coenia*)
Red Bay (*Persea borbonia*)	Palamedes Swallowtail (*Papilio palamedes*)
	Spicebush Swallowtail (*Papilio troilus*)
Rue (*Ruta graveolens*)	Black Swallowtail (*Papilio polyxenes*)
	Giant Swallowtail (*Papilio cresphontes*)
Ruellia (*Ruellia* sp.)	Buckeye (*Junonia coenia*)
	Malachite (*Siproeta stelenes*)
	White Peacock (*Anartia jatrophae*)
Saltwort (*Batis* sp.)	Great Southern White (*Ascia monuste*)
Sassafras (*Sassafras albidum*)	Spicebush Swallowtail (*Papilio troilus*)
Shepherd's Needle (*Bidens alba*)	Dainty Sulphur (*Nathalis iole*)
Slippery Elm (*Ulmus rubra*)	Question Mark (*Polygonia interrogationis*)
Smooth Water Hyssop (*Bacopa monnieri*)	White Peacock (*Anartia jatrophe*)
Southern Red Cedar (*Juniperus virginiana*)	Swedner's Hairstreak (*Mitoura gryneus swedneri*)
Spicebush (*Lindera benzoin*)	Spicebush Swallowtail (*Papilio troilus*)
Sugarberry (*Celtis laevigata*)	Hackberry Butterfly (*Asterocampa celtis*)
	Tawny Emperor (*Asterocampa clyton*)
	Question Mark (*Polygonia interrogationis*)
	Snout Butterfly (*Libytheana bachmanii*)

Swamp Bay (*Persea palustris*)	Palamedes Swallowtail (*Papilio palamedes*) Spicebush Swallowtail (*Papilio troilus*)
Sweet Bay (*Magnolia virginiana*)	Tiger Swallowtail (*Papilio glaucus*) Palamedes Swallowtail (*Papilio palamedes*) Spicebush Swallowtail (*Papilio troilus*)
Toadflax (*Linaria* sp.)	Buckeye (*Junonia coenia*)
Tree Pawpaw (*Asimina triloba*)	Zebra Swallowtail (*Eurytides marcellus*)
Turkey Oak (*Quercus laevis*)	Banded Hairstreak (*Satyrium calanus*)
Virginia Snakeroot (*Aristolochia serpentaria*)	Pipevine Swallowtail (*Battus philenor*) Polydamus Swallowtail (*Battus polydamus*)
Virginia Peppergrass (*Lipidium virginicum*)	Checkered White (*Pontia protodice*) Great Southern White (*Ascia monuste*) Cabbage White (*Pieris rapae*)
Wax Myrtle (*Myrica cerifera*)	Red-banded Hairstreak (*Calycopis cecrops*)
White Oak (*Quercus alba*)	Banded Hairstreak (*Satyrium calanus*)
White Ash (*Fraxinus americana*)	Tiger Swallowtail (*Papilio glaucus*)
White Sweet Clover (*Melilotus alba*)	Gray Hairstreak (*Strymon melinus*) Alfalfa Butterfly (*Colias eurytheme*)
Wild Lime (*Zanthoxylum fagara*)	Giant Swallowtail (*Papilio cresphontes*)
Winged Elm (*Ulmus alata*)	Question Mark (*Polygonia interrogationis*)
Winged Sumac (*Rhus copallina*)	Red-banded Hairstreak (*Calycopis cecrops*)